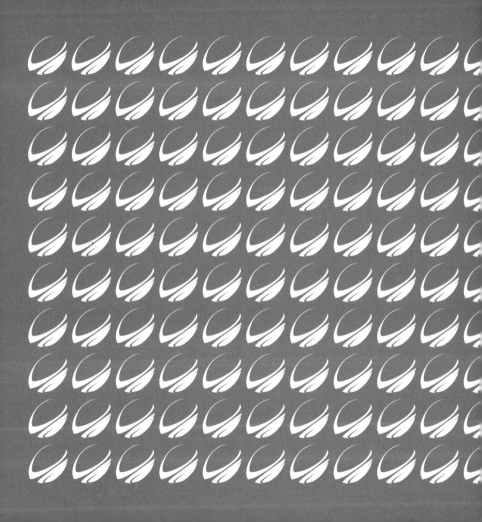

RUGBY

LET'S GET QUIZZICAL

GWION PRYDDERCH

RUGBY: LET'S GET QUIZZICAL
COPYRIGHT © GWION PRYDDERCH, 2014
ALL RIGHTS RESERVED.

NO PART OF THIS BOOK MAY BE REPRODUCED BY ANY MEANS, NOR TRANSMITTED, NOR
TRANSLATED INTO A MACHINE LANGUAGE, WITHOUT THE WRITTEN
PERMISSION OF THE PUBLISHERS.

GWION PRYDDERCH HAS ASSERTED HIS RIGHT TO BE IDENTIFIED AS THE AUTHOR OF THIS WORK IN
ACCORDANCE WITH SECTIONS 77 AND 78 OF THE COPYRIGHT,
DESIGNS AND PATENTS ACT 1988.

CONDITION OF SALE
THIS BOOK IS SOLD SUBJECT TO THE CONDITION THAT IT SHALL NOT, BY WAY OF TRADE OR
OTHERWISE, BE LENT, RE-SOLD, HIRED OUT OR OTHERWISE CIRCULATED IN ANY FORM OF
BINDING OR COVER OTHER THAN THAT IN WHICH IT IS PUBLISHED AND WITHOUT A SIMILAR
CONDITION INCLUDING THIS CONDITION BEING IMPOSED ON THE SUBSEQUENT PURCHASER.

SUMMERSDALE PUBLISHERS LTD
46 WEST STREET
CHICHESTER
WEST SUSSEX
PO19 1RP
UK

WWW.SUMMERSDALE.COM
PRINTED AND BOUND IN CHINA
ISBN: 978-1-84953-612-7

SUBSTANTIAL DISCOUNTS ON BULK QUANTITIES OF SUMMERSDALE BOOKS
ARE AVAILABLE TO CORPORATIONS, PROFESSIONAL ASSOCIATIONS AND OTHER
ORGANISATIONS. FOR DETAILS CONTACT NICKY DOUGLAS BY TELEPHONE:
+44 (0) 1243 756902, FAX: +44 (0) 1243 786300 OR EMAIL: NICKY@SUMMERSDALE.COM

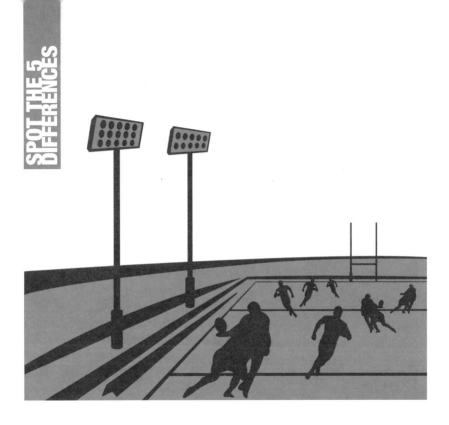

THIS PAIR ONLY APPEARS ONCE
ON THE OPPOSITE PAGE

WHEN WAS A NATIONAL ANTHEM FIRST SUNG BEFORE AN INTERNATIONAL RUGBY MATCH?

A) 1905 (WALES V. NEW ZEALAND)

B) 1921 (ENGLAND V. SCOTLAND)

C) 1947 (IRELAND V. FRANCE)

ALL BLACKS
BARBARIANS
ISLANDERS
JAGUARS
LEOPARDS
LES BLEUS
LIONS
PUMAS
SPRINGBOKS
WALLABIES

```
C S L E O P A R D S
W U Y A U R L M K N
A E M B Y T L O S A
L L I O N S B J A I
L B P P R G L A E R
A S V U N S A G I A
B E T I M V C U O B
I L R W A A K A G R
E P Y Z R O S R N A
S R E D N A L S I B
```

RIP
MRS LYNDON

RICHARD LYNDON MADE RUGBY BALLS FOR RUGBY SCHOOL DURING THE 1850s, HOW DID HIS WIFE DIE?

A) TRIPPED OVER A RUGBY BALL AND HIT HER HEAD

B) INHALING AIR FROM A DISEASED PIG'S BLADDER

C) TRAMPLED BY CATTLE WHILE WATCHING HER HUSBAND PLAY RUGBY

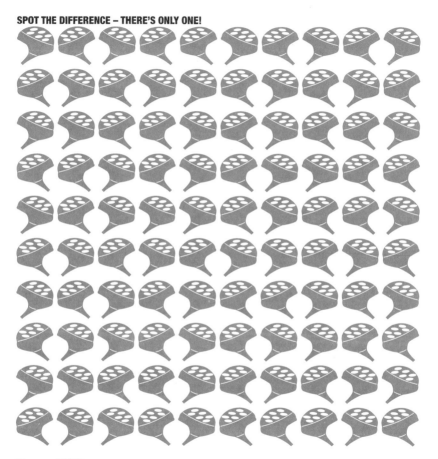

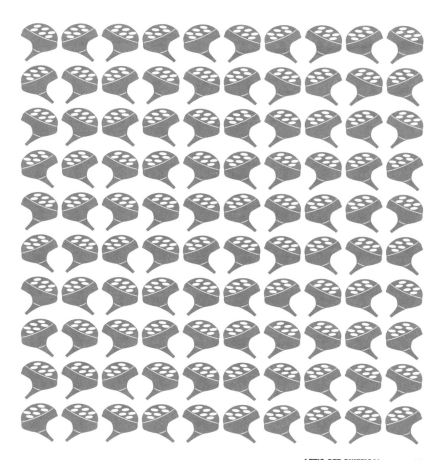

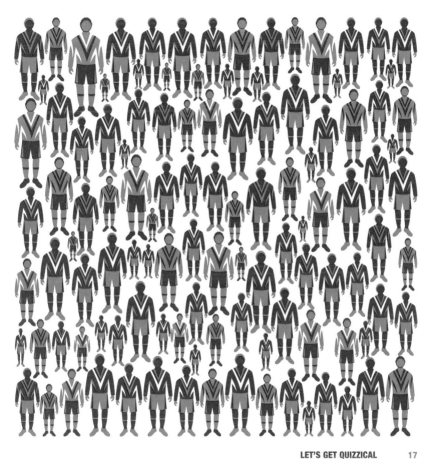

HOW MUCH DOES IT COST TO OPEN THE ROOF OF THE MILLENNIUM STADIUM IN CARDIFF?

A) £2.54

B) £25.40

C) £254.00

THIS PAIR ONLY APPEARS ONCE ON THE OPPOSITE PAGE

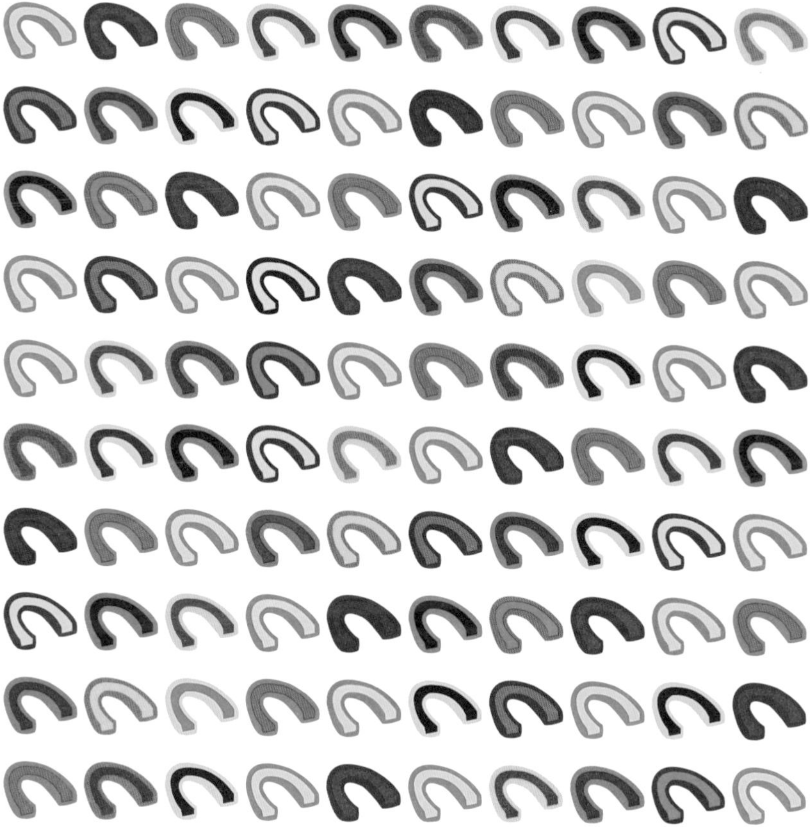

WE CAN'T SCRUMMAGE WITHOUT OUR TIGHT-HEAD PROP, CAN YOU FIND HIM?

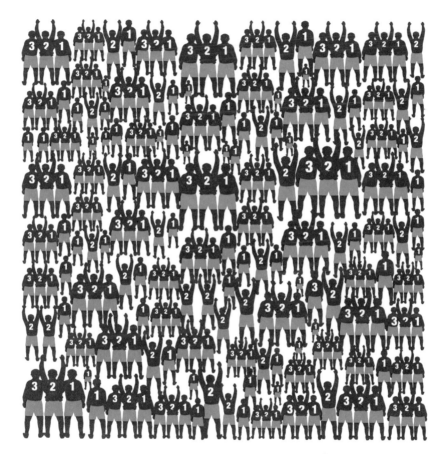

THIS PAIR ONLY APPEARS ONCE
ON THE OPPOSITE PAGE

THE GIL EVANS WHISTLE IS USED TO KICK OFF THE OPENING GAME OF EVERY RUGBY WORLD CUP TOURNAMENT, BUT WHEN WAS IT FIRST USED?

A) 1896 (IRELAND V. SCOTLAND)

B) 1905 (ENGLAND V. NEW ZEALAND)

C) 1922 (AUSTRALIA V. NEW ZEALAND)

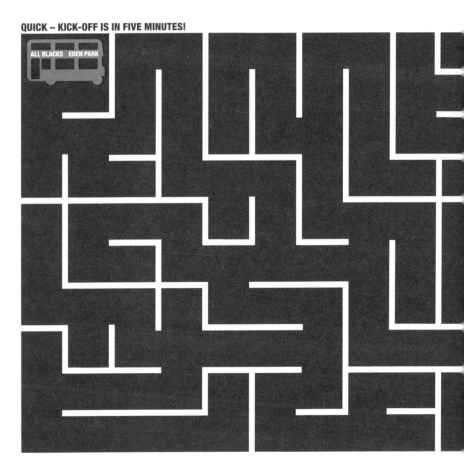

WHICH IS THE WORLD'S OLDEST SURVIVING RUGBY CLUB?

A) BLACKHEATH FOOTBALL CLUB

B) DUBLIN UNIVERSITY FOOTBALL CLUB

C) HARLEQUINS FOOTBALL CLUB

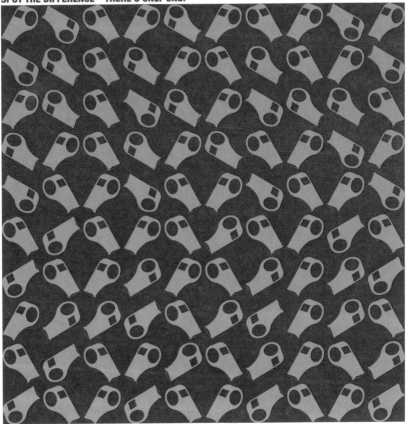

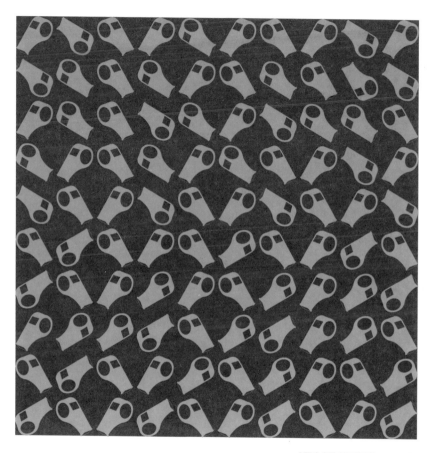

WHO WON THE LAST OLYMPIC RUGBY GOLD MEDAL IN 1924?

A) THE UNITED STATES

B) FRANCE

C) GREAT BRITAIN

WHICH OF THESE COUNTRIES HAS RUGBY LEAGUE AS ITS NATIONAL SPORT?

A) NEW ZEALAND

B) MADAGASCAR

C) PAPUA NEW GUINEA

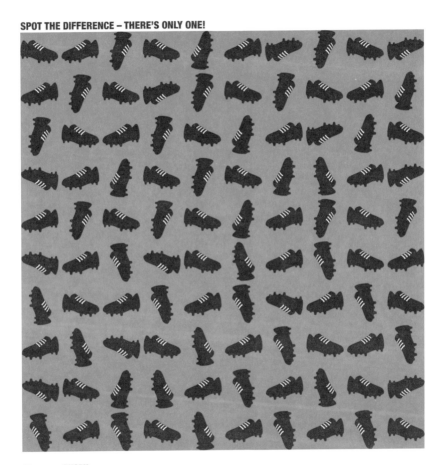

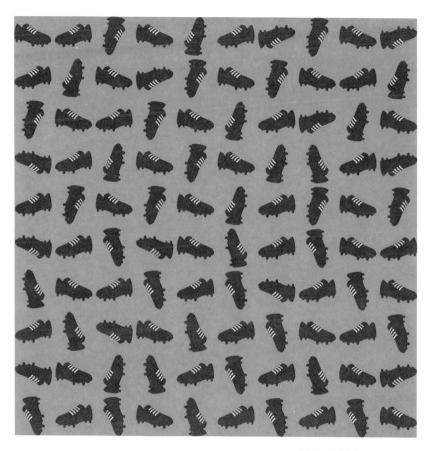

**THIS PAIR ONLY APPEARS ONCE
ON THE OPPOSITE PAGE**

'FLOWER OF' (SCOTLAND)
'SIVA TAU' (SAMOA)
'WILD ROVER' (IRELAND)
'CALON LÂN' (WALES)
'CIBI' (FIJI)
'SWING LOW' (ENGLAND)
'WALTZING' (MATILDA) (AUSTRALIA)
'THE HAKA' (NEW ZEALAND)
'SIPI TAU' (TONGA)
'DIE STEM' (SOUTH AFRICA)

```
R  K  W  P  N  R  N  M  S  M
E  D  A  A  A  U  L  V  T  E
V  C  K  R  L  A  T  I  W  T
O  B  A  C  N  T  B  O  O  S
R  A  H  E  O  I  Z  I  L  E
D  I  E  O  L  P  B  I  G  I
L  U  H  D  A  I  F  G  N  D
I  Y  T  R  C  S  L  H  I  G
W  S  I  V  A  T  A  U  W  C
F  L  O  W  E  R  O  F  S  I
```

KNOCK ON **BALL NOT RELEASED** **FREE KICK** **PENALTY**

**LINE-OUT THROW
NOT STRAIGHT**   **TRY**   **OBSTRUCTION**   **FORWARD
PASS**

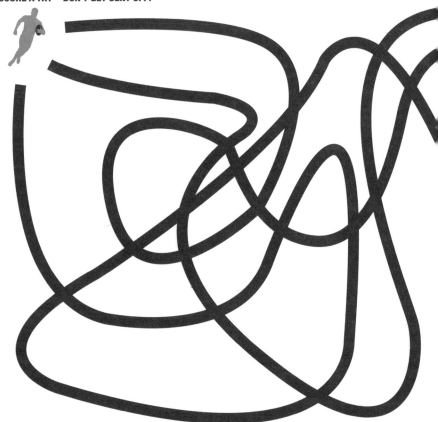

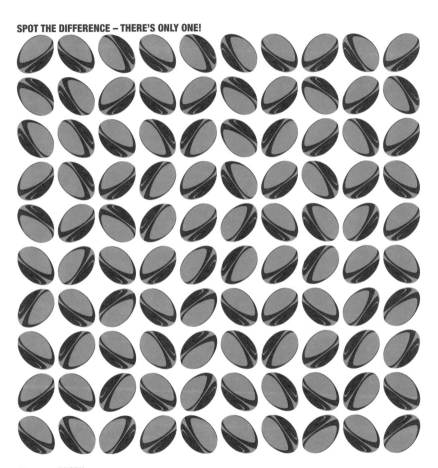

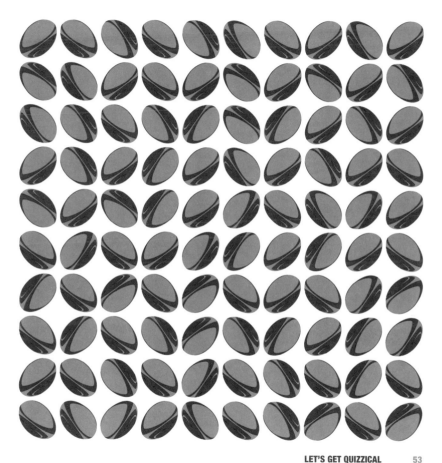

THIS PAIR ONLY APPEARS ONCE
ON THE OPPOSITE PAGE

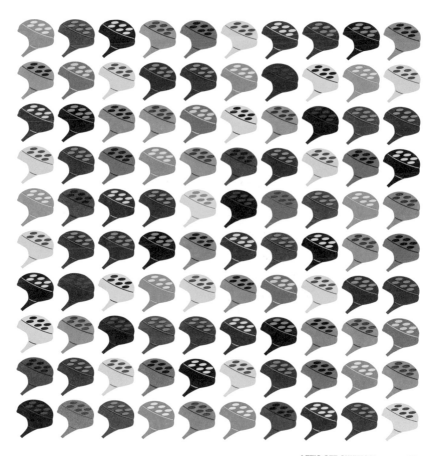

IN WHAT YEAR DID THE RUGBY FOOTBALL UNION OFFICIALLY ENDORSE THE NOW ICONIC OVAL-SHAPED BALL?

A) 1885

B) 1892

C) 1902

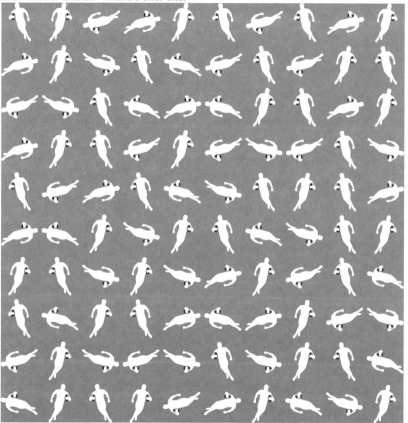

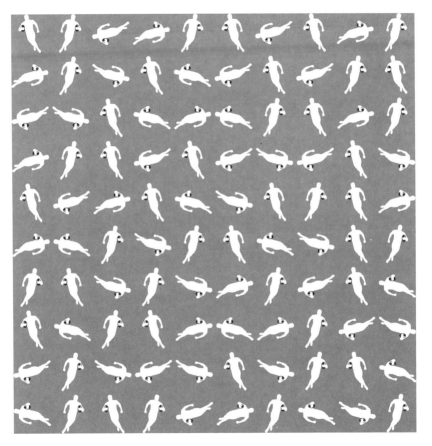

THIS PAIR ONLY APPEARS ONCE
ON THE OPPOSITE PAGE

WELCOME TO ANAGRAM RFC — CAN YOU WORK OUT THE TEAM SHEET?

PROP
SOUTH AFRICA

RUN AT ODDS

1

HOOKER
IRELAND

HOOKED WIT

2

PROP
NEW ZEALAND

CAN LAY HARM

3

LOCK
AUSTRALIA

JEANS HOLE

4

LOCK
SOUTH AFRICA

SHAKE A KIT BOB

5

FLANKER
FRANCE

I HIT DOUR TREASURY

6

NUMBER EIGHT
ITALY

PIE IS A GROSSER

8

FLANKER
SCOTLAND

FAIRLY LANCED

7

RIGHT WING
AUSTRALIA

EVADES
MID CAP

14

FULL-BACK
FRANCE

CLEANERS
BOG

15

LEFT WING
WALES

WE IN A
SMALLISH

11

CENTRE
IRELAND

CLARION
BOLD SIR

13

CENTRE
NEW ZEALAND

AM A
NOUN

12

OUTSIDE-HALF
ENGLAND

WINK JOINS
NYLON

10

SCRUM-HALF
ARGENTINA

TOUCHING
PAS IT

9

THE CLOCK'S TURNED RED AND YOU'RE TWO POINTS BEHIND!

IN 2003, 142–0 BECAME THE BIGGEST-EVER WINNING MARGIN IN A RUGBY WORLD CUP MATCH – BETWEEN WHICH TWO NATIONS?

A) NEW ZEALAND AND JAPAN

B) AUSTRALIA AND NAMIBIA

C) SOUTH AFRICA AND GEORGIA

FIND THE WHITE RUGBY SHOE!

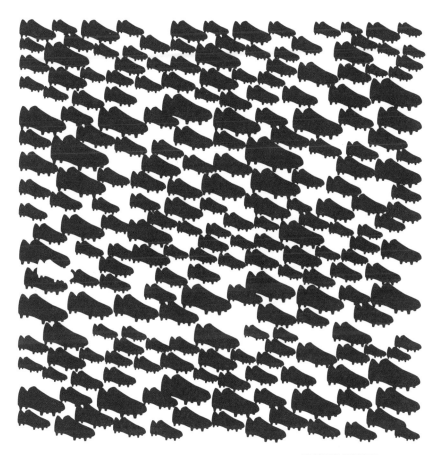

BALL

POSTS

SHIRT

SCRUM CAP

GUMSHIELD

BOOTS

HEADBAND

SOCKS

WHISTLE

CORNER FLAG

SHORTS

TIE-UPS

```
S H I R T A W B G C
D P E U I L H H A O
S G U M S H I E L D
H C F E S O S A F R
O S R K I T T D R I
R T C U S T L B E E
T O B O M N E A N S
S O P A T C U N R O
G B K M L V A D O A
H I J L W L Y P C P
```

HOW MANY WOMEN'S RUGBY WORLD CUPS WERE HELD BEFORE THEY BECAME OFFICIALLY SANCTIONED BY THE INTERNATIONAL RUGBY BOARD?

A) ONE

B) TWO

C) THREE

**THIS PAIR ONLY APPEARS ONCE
ON THE OPPOSITE PAGE**

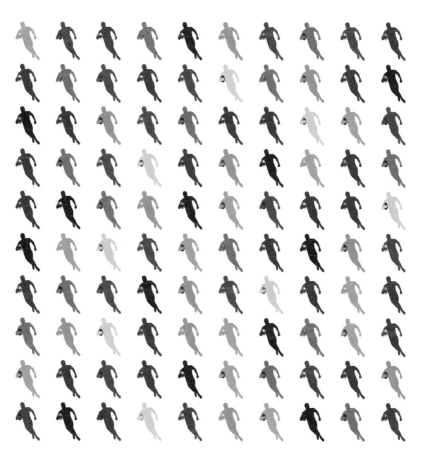

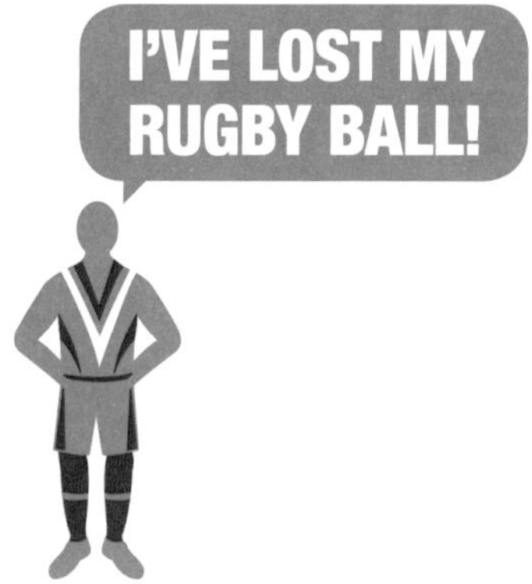
I'VE LOST MY RUGBY BALL!

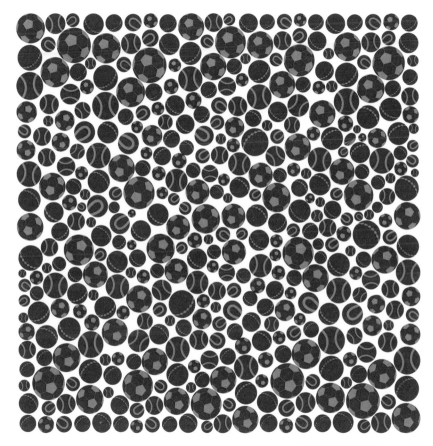

WHO SAID 'YOU'VE GOT TO GET YOUR FIRST TACKLE IN EARLY, EVEN IF IT'S LATE'?

A) BRIAN MOORE

B) DAVID CAMPESE

C) RAY GRAVELL

**THIS PAIR ONLY APPEARS ONCE
ON THE OPPOSITE PAGE**

MAKE THAT TRY-SAVING TACKLE!

HOW DID LONDON WASPS MISS OUT ON BEING A FOUNDING MEMBER OF THE RFU?

A) THEIR REP WAS GIVEN THE WRONG TIME, ADDRESS AND DATE FOR THE INAUGURAL MEETING

B) THEY DIDN'T EXIST AS A TEAM UNTIL FIVE YEARS AFTER THE RFU WAS FORMED

C) THEY WEREN'T ABLE TO MAKE THE MONETARY CONTRIBUTION REQUIRED TO JOIN THE SOCIETY

IN 1991 VA'AIGA TUIGAMALA MADE HIS DEBUT FOR NEW ZEALAND. HIS LAST CAP WAS IN 2001, BUT FOR WHICH COUNTRY?

A) FIJI

B) SAMOA

C) TONGA

**THIS PAIR ONLY APPEARS ONCE
ON THE OPPOSITE PAGE**

S_____ S_____ GLASGOW WARRIORS

S_____ S_____ WORCESTER WARRIORS

K_____ S_____ GLOUCESTER

R_____ P_____ NEWPORT DRAGONS

C_____ A___ P___ CARDIFF BLUES

P___ Y S_____ SCARLETS

L_____ S_____ OSPREYS

S____ P___ EXETER CHIEFS

T__ R__ BATH

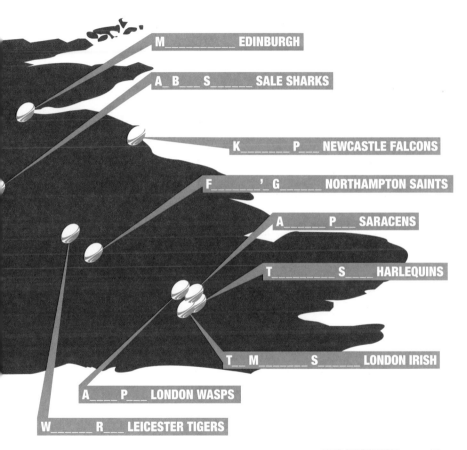

M_____ EDINBURGH

A_B____ S_____ SALE SHARKS

K_____ P____ NEWCASTLE FALCONS

F_____' G_____ NORTHAMPTON SAINTS

A_____ P____ SARACENS

T_____ S____ HARLEQUINS

T__ M____ S____ LONDON IRISH

A_____ P____ LONDON WASPS

W_____ R____ LEICESTER TIGERS

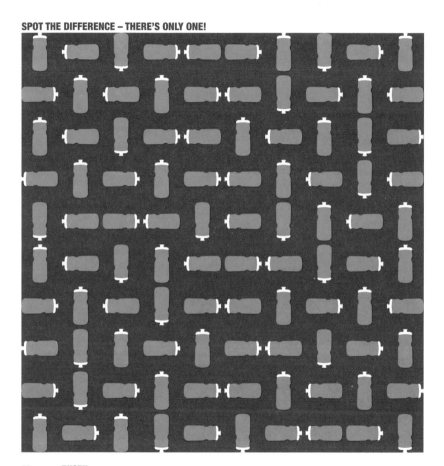

IN 2000 NEW ZEALAND BEAT AUSTRALIA IN FRONT OF THE LARGEST RECORDED CROWD AT AN INTERNATIONAL RUGBY MATCH. HOW MANY PEOPLE WERE THERE?

A) 89,726

B) 99,327

C) 109,874

BURKE (MATT, MAY 2004 V. WAL)
MARSHALL (JUSTIN, DEC 2004 V. NZ)
REGAN (MARK, DEC 2007 V. SA)
TURINUI (MORGAN, MAY 2008 V. IRE)
CORRY (MARTIN, MAY 2009 V. ENG)
WAUGH (PHIL, JUN 2009 V. AUS)
RUSH (XAVIER, JUN 2010 V. IRE)
GITEAU (MATT, DEC 2010 V. SA)
MATFIELD (VICTOR, NOV 2011 V. AUS)
SMIT (JOHN, JUN 2012 V. WAL)
TINDALL (MIKE, MAY 2013 V. ENG)
PARISSE (SERGIO, JUN 2013 V. LIONS)

```
V H L I N L J T O K
H D M A T F I E L D
G B G F C M U H L L
U E E H S A N M A L
A A S P E A I Y H A
W U S T G R R E S D
R S I E O R U K R N
T G R I O U T R A I
L T A C B A Y U M T
E F P N M R V B W U
```

ANSWERS

P4-5

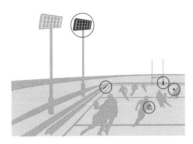

P10-11

P12-13 B) INHALING AIR FROM A DISEASED PIG'S BLADDER

P6-7

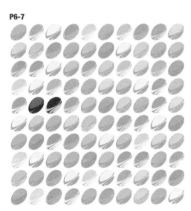

P14-15

P16-17

P22-23

P18-19 A) £2.54

P20-21

P24-25

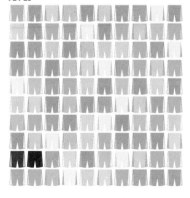

P36-37 A) UNITED STATES

P38-39

P40-41 C) PAPUA NEW GUINEA

P42-43

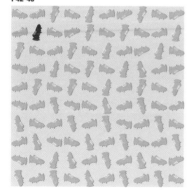

P44-45

P46-47

| PENALTY | FREE KICK | KNOCK ON | TRY | FORWARD PASS | OBSTRUCTION | BALL NOT RELEASED | LINE-OUT THROW NOT STRAIGHT |

P52-53

P54-55

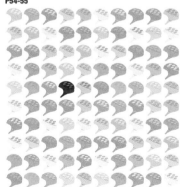

P56-57 B) 1892

P58-59

P60-61

P62-63

PROP
SOUTH AFRICA
OS DU RANDT
1

HOOKER
IRELAND
KEITH WOOD
2

PROP
NEW ZELAND
CARL HAYMAN
3

LOCK
AUSTRALIA
JOHN EALES
4

LOCK
SOUTH AFRICA
BAKKIES BOTHA
5

FLANKER
FRANCE
THIERRY DUSAUTOIR
6

NUMBER EIGHT
ITALY
SERGIO PARISSE
8

FLANKER
SCOTLAND
FINLAY CALDER
7

RIGHT WING
AUSTRALIA
DAVID CAMPESE
14

FULL-BACK
FRANCE
SERGE BLANCO
15

LEFT WING
WALES
SHANE WILLIAMS
11

CENTRE
IRELAND
BRIAN O'DRISCOLL
13

CENTRE
NEW ZELAND
MA'A NONU
12

OUTSIDE-HALF
ENGLAND
JONNY WILKINSON
10

SCRUM-HALF
ARGENTINA
AGUSTÍN PICHOT
9

P66-67 B) AUSTRALIA AND NAMIBIA

P64-65

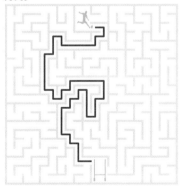

P68-69

P70-71

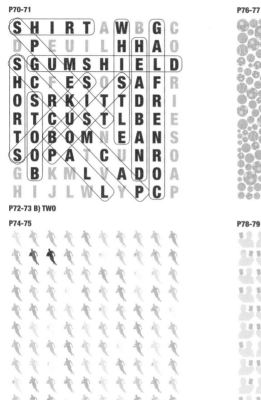

P72-73 B) TWO

P74-75

P76-77

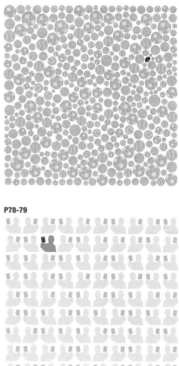

P78-79

P80-81 C) RAY GRAVELL

P82-83

P84-85

P86-87 A) THEIR REP WAS GIVEN THE WRONG TIME, ADDRESS AND DATE FOR THE INAUGURAL MEETING

P88-89

P90-91 B) SAMOA

P92-93

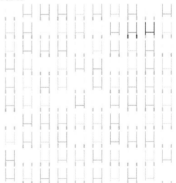

P94-95

SCOTSTOUN STADIUM GLASGOW WARRIORS

MURRAYFIELD EDINBURGH

SIXWAYS STADIUM WORCESTER WARRIORS

AJ BELL STADIUM SALE SHARKS

KINGSHOLM STADIUM GLOUCESTER

KINGSTON PARK NEWCASTLE FALCONS

RODNEY PARADE NEWPORT DRAGONS

FRANKLIN'S GARDENS NORTHAMPTON SAINTS

CARDIFF ARMS PARK CARDIFF BLUES

ALLIANZ PARK SARACENS

PARC Y SCARLETS SCARLETS

TWICKENHAM STOOP HARLEQUINS

LIBERTY STADIUM OSPREYS

THE MADEJSKI STADIUM LONDON IRISH

ADAMS PARK LONDON WASPS

SANDY PARK EXETER CHIEFS   THE REC BATH   WELFORD ROAD LEICESTER TIGERS

P98-99 C) 109,874

P96-97

P100-101

LET'S GET QUIZZICAL 111

IF YOU'RE INTERESTED IN FINDING OUT MORE ABOUT OUR BOOKS,
FIND US ON FACEBOOK AT SUMMERSDALE PUBLISHERS AND
FOLLOW US ON TWITTER AT @SUMMERSDALE.

WWW.SUMMERSDALE.COM

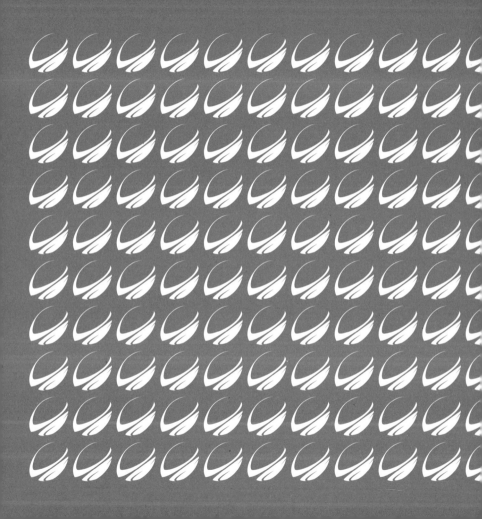